NATIONAL GEOGRAPHIC

T0040369

Animals All Together

Dominic Loughrey

Four otters sit on the rocks.

Two otters swim in the water.

How many otters all together?

4 + 2 =

Six zebras run across the grass.

Six zebras drink from the river.

How many zebras all together?

6 + 6 =

One whale swims in the sea.

Five whales jump out of the water.
How many whales all together?
1 + 5 =

Six penguins walk in the snow.

Three penguins dive off the ice.

How many penguins all together?

6 + 3 =

Five elephants walk on the grass.

Six elephants drink from the river.

How many elephants all together?

5 + 6 =

Animals All Together

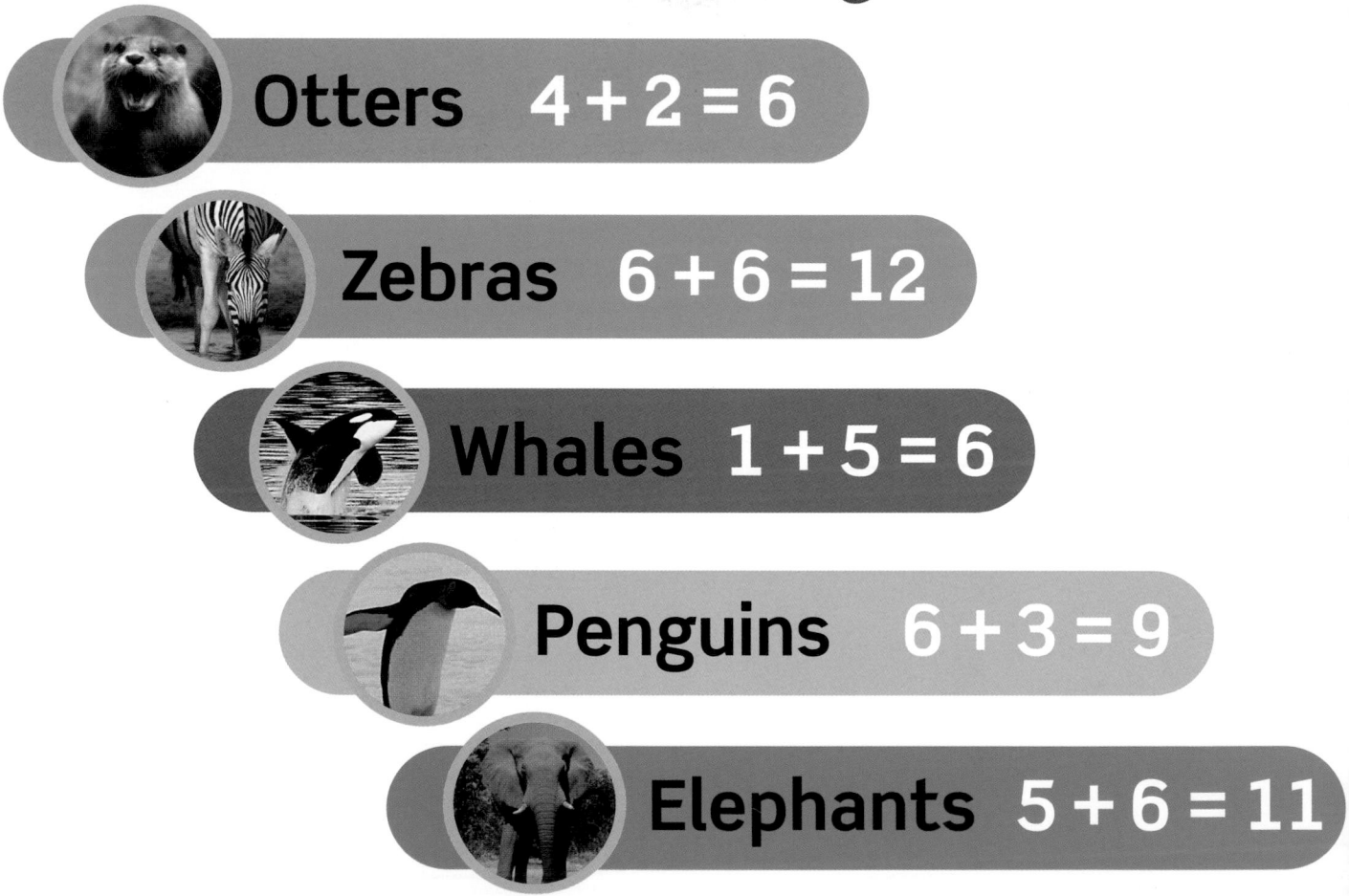